THE INDIAN KITCHEN

A GASTRONOMICAL JOURNEY THROUGH INDIA'S REGIONAL CUISINES

DR. JAGADEESH PILLAI

|| Dedicated to Wisdom Seekers Around The World ||

Contents

Contents

Prayer

"Om Asato Maa Sadgamaya, Tamaso Maa Jyotir Gamaya, Mrityor Maa Amritam Gamaya, Om Shantih, Shantih, Shantih"

The true meaning of this mantra is: OM guide me from the unreal to the real, from darkness to light, and from mortality to immortality.
OM Peace, Peace, Peace.

❦❦❦

About The Author

Dr. Jagadeesh Pillai is a renowned Guinness World Record holder, writer, and researcher hailing from Varanasi, also known as the abode of Lord Shiva. With a Ph.D. in Vedic Science and a range of creative ideas and achievements, he is a true polymath. He is the author of more than 100 books including Research Publications. Although his roots can be traced back to Kerala, the people of Varanasi hold him in high regard and affectionately consider him one of their own.

Dr. Pillai has achieved four Guinness World Records in the following subjects:

"Script to Screen" - In this record, Dr. Pillai produced and directed an animation film within the shortest time possible, breaking the previous record set by Canadians. He has also received numerous national and international awards and recognitions for this achievement.

Longest Line of Postcards - For this record, Dr. Pillai created a line of 16,300 postcards on the occasion of the 163rd anniversary of Indian Postal Day. The event also included a questionnaire about the Indian flag.

Largest Poster Awareness Campaign - Dr. Pillai designed an awareness campaign on the subject of "Beti Bachao - Beti Padhao" (Save the Girl Child - Educate the Girl Child) to achieve this record.

Largest Envelope - In tribute to the Indian Prime Minister's

"Make in India" initiative, Dr. Pillai created a 4000 square meter envelope using waste paper to achieve this record.

Attempted - **70000 Candles on a 210 kg Cake** - To celebrate the 70th Indian Independence Day, Dr. Pillai attempted to light 70,000 candles on a 210 kg cake, which was recorded in World Records India.

Attempted - **Documentary on Dhamek Stupa of Sarnath in 17 Languages** - Dr. Pillai attempted to create a documentary on the Dhamek Stupa of Sarnath, dubbing it in 17 different languages. The result of this attempt is currently awaiting confirmation from the Guinness World Records.

Dr. Pillai is skilled in teaching the Bhagavad Gita, a Hindu scripture, and is popular among young people. He has helped many young people improve their lives through his motivational teachings.

In addition to teaching, he has composed and sung numerous Sanskrit Bhajans and patriotic songs.

He has also written and directed several short films and documentaries for awareness campaigns, and has volunteered with the police in both UP and Kerala to spread awareness about various issues through videos and photography.

Incredibly, he has produced and directed over 100 documentaries about the city of Varanasi, all on his own.

He has also helped and guided more than 25 boys and girls to achieve world records through creative and innovative methods. He is a multifaceted person who uses his intellect and the blessings given to him by God to excel in various areas. He is both a teacher and a student, always learning and teaching, and is able to master any subject he comes across.

He is a selfless social activist and motivational speaker who has overcome struggles and failures to become a successful and enthusiastic individual with a rich life experience.

In addition to his work with the Bhagavad Gita, he is also an efficient Tarot card reader, Astro-Vastu consultant, and a talented singer and composer. He has sung the entire Ram Charita Manas and Bhagavad Gita in his own compositions, and has sung the phrase "Lokah Samastha Sukhino Bhavantu" in 50 different languages. He is currently working on a detailed and scientific study of Vedas, Upanishads, Puranas, and the Bhagavad Gita. He has also composed and sung the Hanuman Chalisa and Gayatri Mantra in 108 and 1008 different compositions, respectively.

Awards - Four Times Guinness World Records, Winner of Mahatma Gandhi Vishwa Shanti Puraskar, Mahatma Gandhi Global Peace Ambassador, Kashi Ratna Award, Dr. APJ Abdul Kalam Motivational Person of the Year 2017, Mother Teresa Award, Indira Gandhi Priyadarshini Award, Bharat Vikas Ratna Award, Udyog Ratna Award, Vigyan Prasar Award, Poorvanchal Ratn Samman.

ॐॐॐ

Preface

The Indian Kitchen: A Gastronomical Journey Through India's Regional Cuisines is a comprehensive guide to the diverse and vibrant world of Indian cuisine. This book takes readers on a journey through the different regions of India, exploring the unique ingredients, cooking techniques, and flavors that define each area's culinary heritage.

From the rich and flavorful dishes of the North, to the spicy and tangy delicacies of the South, this book delves into the history and philosophy of Indian cuisine, providing a deep understanding of the cultural and religious influences that have shaped it.

In this book, readers will discover the evolution of Indian spices and seasonings, the diverse street foods and snacks, and the regional drinks and beverages that make Indian cuisine so unique. The book also explores the impact of the Mughal Empire on Indian cuisine, and how Indian food has influenced global cuisine.

With chapters on the diversity of Indian cuisine, the relationship between Indian cuisine and religion, and the fast-evolving modern cuisine scene in India, this book is an essential guide for anyone who wants to discover the flavors and traditions of India's regional cuisines.

Whether you're a food lover, a chef, or a traveler, this book will take you on a culinary journey through the different regions of India, providing a deeper understanding and appreciation of the country's rich culinary heritage.

This book is a perfect guide for anyone who wants to discover the flavors and traditions of India's regional cuisines. It provides a comprehensive overview of the history, philosophy and cultural influences of Indian cuisine, with a focus on the traditional ingredients, cooking techniques, and flavors that define each region. The book also covers the fast-evolving modern cuisine scene in India, and how Indian food has influenced global cuisine. It's an essential guide for food enthusiasts and travelers, and anyone who is interested in discovering the rich and diverse culinary heritage of India.

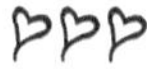

ONE

THE DIVERSITY OF INDIAN CUISINE

Indian cuisine is renowned for its diversity, with a wide variety of dishes and flavors that reflect the country's rich cultural heritage. The Indian kitchen is a melting pot of ingredients, techniques, and traditions from various regions of the country, each with its unique culinary identity.

The history of Indian cuisine can be traced back to ancient times, when the Indus Valley Civilization developed a sophisticated system of agriculture and food production. Over the centuries, Indian cuisine has been influenced by a variety of cultures, including the Mughals, the British, and the Portuguese. This has resulted in a rich and diverse culinary tradition that is celebrated across the world.

The diversity of Indian cuisine is reflected in the wide range of regional cuisines that can be found throughout the country. Each region has its own unique culinary identity, shaped by its climate, geography, and cultural heritage. For example, the coastal regions of India are known for their seafood dishes, while the northern regions are famous for their rich and creamy curries.

The Indian Kitchen: A Gastronomical Journey Through India's Regional Cuisines explores the diversity of Indian cuisine through a tour of the country's different regions and their culinary traditions. From the spicy curries of the South to the tandoori dishes of the North, this book offers a comprehensive and delicious tour of Indian cuisine.

The book is organized by region, with each chapter focusing on a specific area of the country and its unique culinary traditions. The chapters include information on the ingredients, techniques, and dishes that are characteristic of each region, as well as traditional recipes that have been passed down through generations.

Indian cuisine. Whether you're a food lover, a home cook, or a professional chef, this book will take you on a journey through the vibrant and delicious world of Indian cuisine. With detailed information on the ingredients, techniques, and dishes of each region, this book is an invaluable resource for anyone interested in exploring the many flavors and traditions of Indian cuisine.

Throughout the book, you will discover the unique and delicious regional dishes of India, from the rich and creamy curries of the North to the spicy and flavorful seafood dishes of the South. You will also learn about the cultural and historical influences that have shaped Indian cuisine and the traditional cooking techniques that are still used today.

In addition to traditional recipes, the book also includes modern twists on classic dishes, offering a contemporary take on Indian cuisine. This allows readers to explore the diversity of Indian cuisine in a new and exciting way.

This book is not only a culinary guide but also a cultural journey through India's rich and diverse culinary traditions. It is an invitation to discover the flavors, ingredients, and techniques of India's regional cuisines and to explore the unique tastes and aromas that make Indian food so special and beloved around the world.

Indian cuisine is renowned for its diversity, reflecting the country's rich cultural heritage and history. The Indian Kitchen: A Gastronomical Journey Through India's Regional Cuisines offers a comprehensive and delicious tour of Indian cuisine, exploring the unique culinary traditions and flavors of each region. This book is a must-read for anyone interested in discovering the diversity and richness of Indian cuisine.

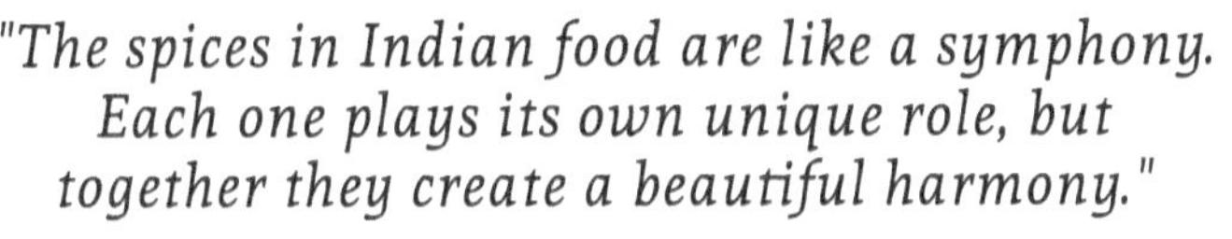

"The spices in Indian food are like a symphony. Each one plays its own unique role, but together they create a beautiful harmony."

TWO

REGIONAL OVERVIEW: NORTH INDIAN CUISINE

North Indian cuisine is known for its rich and flavorful dishes, characterized by the use of creamy gravies, a variety of spices, and a mix of vegetarian and non-vegetarian options. The cuisine of this region is heavily influenced by the Mughal Empire, which ruled over large parts of North India for centuries, and has a strong Persian influence.

One of the most iconic dishes of North Indian cuisine is the tandoori chicken, which is marinated in a blend of yogurt, spices, and lemon juice, and then cooked in a clay oven known as a tandoor. Other popular non-vegetarian dishes include kebabs, biryani, and butter chicken.

Vegetarian dishes are also an important part of North

Indian cuisine. Some of the most popular vegetarian dishes include dal makhani, chana masala, and palak paneer, which is spinach cooked with cubes of cottage cheese. North Indian cuisine also features a variety of breads such as naan, roti, and paratha, which are often served with curries and gravies.

North Indian cuisine is also famous for its rich and creamy gravies, which are often made with a variety of nuts and spices, such as cashews and cardamom. Ghee, a clarified butter, is also commonly used in North Indian cooking to add a rich and buttery flavor to dishes.

One of the most iconic culinary traditions of North Indian cuisine is the "dhaba" culture, where a dhaba is a roadside restaurant that serves traditional North Indian food, often with a rustic and hearty feel.

Dhaba culture is a hallmark of Northern Indian cuisine. For those unfamiliar, dhabas are casual eateries typically found in small towns or on highways throughout India where fresh, homemade food is prepared for travelers. Dhabas offer rustic menu items such as tandoori roti breads, spiced lentils and chickpeas known as dal chawal, and various curries amongst other dishes that vary from region to region. Offering hot tea and chai infused with cardamom, these roadside restaurants provide affordable prices along with a gregarious atmosphere stemming from their camaraderie-encouraging communal seating setups that bring people together over the joys of simple home-cooked meals. As you set out on your next journey through Northern India be sure to pop into one of the lively local dhabas for an appetizing and authentic experience filled with flavorful spices!

North Indian cuisine is known for its rich and flavorful dishes, characterized by the use of creamy gravies, a variety of spices, and a mix of vegetarian and non-vegetarian options. The cuisine of this region is heavily influenced by the Mughal Empire and has a strong Persian influence. North Indian cuisine includes iconic dishes such as tandoori chicken, kebabs, biryani, and butter chicken and popular vegetarian dishes such as dal makhani, chana masala, and palak paneer. It also features a variety of breads and rich and creamy gravies, often made with nuts and spices.

"An Indian kitchen is not just a place to cook,
it's a place where memories are made and love
is shared."

THREE

REGIONAL OVERVIEW: SOUTH INDIAN CUISINE

South Indian cuisine is known for its unique flavors and use of a wide variety of spices. The cuisine of this region is heavily influenced by the geography, climate, and history of the South Indian states, which include Andhra Pradesh, Tamil Nadu, Kerala, and Karnataka.

One of the most iconic dishes of South Indian cuisine is dosa, a type of fermented pancake made from a batter of rice and lentils. It is often served with a variety of chutneys and sambar, a lentil-based stew. Other popular dishes include idli, a steamed rice and lentil cake, and uttapam, a thicker version of dosa with vegetables mixed into the batter.

South Indian cuisine also features a variety of curries and gravies, often made with coconut milk and a blend of spices such as mustard seeds, curry leaves, and tamarind. Seafood is also a staple in South Indian cuisine, with a wide range of fish and seafood dishes such as fish curry and prawn fry.

Rice is a staple in South Indian cuisine, and is often served with a variety of vegetarian and non-vegetarian dishes. A popular breakfast item is the traditional "Idli-Sambar", which is a steamed rice cake that is often served with lentil stew.

South Indian cuisine also places great emphasis on vegetarianism, and a large proportion of the dishes are vegetarian, making use of a wide variety of vegetables, lentils, and legumes.

South Indian cuisine is known for its unique flavors and use of a wide variety of spices. The cuisine of this region is heavily influenced by the geography, climate, and history of the South Indian states. Iconic dishes of South Indian cuisine include dosa, idli, and uttapam, which are often served with a variety of chutneys and sambar.

The cuisine also features a variety of curries and gravies, often made with coconut milk and a blend of spices, and a wide variety of seafood dishes. Rice is a staple in South Indian cuisine and is often served with both vegetarian and non-vegetarian dishes. Vegetarianism is also an important aspect of South Indian cuisine, with a large proportion of dishes being vegetarian, making use of a wide variety of vegetables, lentils, and legumes. South Indian cuisine is diverse and delicious, offering a unique and exciting culinary experience to anyone who is interested in discovering the flavors and traditions of this region.

"The beauty of Indian food lies in its ability to balance bold flavors and fragrant spices."

FOUR

REGIONAL OVERVIEW: EAST INDIAN CUISINE

East Indian cuisine is known for its unique flavors and use of a wide variety of ingredients. The cuisine of this region is heavily influenced by the geography, climate, and history of the East Indian states, which include Odisha, West Bengal, and Assam.

One of the most iconic dishes of East Indian cuisine is the famous "Dhokla", a steamed savory cake made from fermented rice and lentil batter. It is often served with a variety of chutneys and sambar, a lentil-based stew. Other popular dishes include "Luchi", a deep-fried flatbread, and "Fish curry", a flavorful fish dish that is often made with mustard seeds, ginger, and other spices.

East Indian cuisine also features a variety of curries and gravies, often made with a blend of spices such as ginger, mustard seeds, and curry leaves. The use of mustard oil is also common in East Indian cooking, giving dishes a distinct and pungent flavor.

Rice is also a staple in East Indian cuisine, and is often served with a variety of vegetarian and non-vegetarian dishes. Vegetarian dishes are also an important part of East Indian cuisine, with a wide range of dishes made with lentils, vegetables, and legumes.

East Indian cuisine is known for its unique flavors and use of a wide variety of ingredients. The cuisine of this region is heavily influenced by the geography, climate, and history of the East Indian states. Iconic dishes of East Indian cuisine include Dhokla, Luchi, and Fish curry, which are often served with a variety of chutneys and sambar.

The cuisine also features a variety of curries and gravies, often made with a blend of spices and mustard oil. Rice is a staple in East Indian cuisine, and both vegetarian and non-vegetarian dishes are an important part of the cuisine. The East Indian cuisine offers a unique and exciting culinary experience to anyone who is interested in discovering the flavors and traditions of this region.

ᐳᐳᐳ

"Indian spices are like a journey through the senses. Each one tells its own story and takes you on a different adventure."

FIVE

REGIONAL OVERVIEW: WEST INDIAN CUISINE

West Indian cuisine is known for its rich flavors and use of a wide variety of spices. The cuisine of this region is heavily influenced by the geography, climate, and history of the West Indian states, which include Maharashtra, Gujarat, and Goa.

One of the most iconic dishes of West Indian cuisine is the famous "Vada pav", a popular street food consisting of a deep-fried potato dumpling served in a bun with a variety of chutneys and spices. Another popular dish is "Bhelpuri", a street food made from puffed rice, vegetables, and a variety of chutneys.

West Indian cuisine also features a variety of curries and gravies, often made with a blend of spices such as ginger, garlic, and chili powder. The use of coconut milk is also common in West Indian cooking, giving dishes a rich and creamy texture.

Rice and breads such as roti and puri are also staples in West Indian cuisine, and are often served with a variety of vegetarian and non-vegetarian dishes. Vegetarian dishes are also an important part of West Indian cuisine, with a wide range of dishes made with lentils, vegetables, and legumes.

West Indian cuisine is known for its rich flavors and use of a wide variety of spices. The cuisine of this region is heavily influenced by the geography, climate, and history of the West Indian states. Iconic dishes of West Indian cuisine include Vada pav, Bhelpuri, and a variety of curries and gravies, often made with a blend of spices and coconut milk.

Rice and breads are also staples in West Indian cuisine, and both vegetarian and non-vegetarian dishes are an important part of the cuisine. West Indian cuisine offers a unique and exciting culinary experience to anyone who is interested in discovering the flavors and traditions of this region.

ppp

"In an Indian kitchen, food is not just
sustenance, it's an expression of love and care."

SIX

REGIONAL OVERVIEW: CENTRAL INDIAN CUISINE

Central Indian cuisine is known for its unique flavors and use of a wide variety of spices. The cuisine of this region is heavily influenced by the geography, climate, and history of the central Indian states, which include Madhya Pradesh, Chhattisgarh, and parts of Maharashtra.

One of the most iconic dishes of Central Indian cuisine is the famous "Jalebi", a deep-fried spiral-shaped sweet made from wheat flour and soaked in sugar syrup. Another popular dish is "Samosa", a deep-fried or baked pastry filled with savory fillings such as potatoes and peas.

Central Indian cuisine also features a variety of curries and gravies, often made with a blend of spices such as cumin, coriander, and turmeric. The use of ghee, a clarified butter, is also common in Central Indian cooking, giving dishes a rich and buttery flavor.

Rice and breads such as chapati and bhakri are also staples in Central Indian cuisine, and are often served with a variety of vegetarian and non-vegetarian dishes. Vegetarian dishes are also an important part of Central Indian cuisine, with a wide range of dishes made with lentils, vegetables, and legumes.

Central Indian cuisine is known for its unique flavors and use of a wide variety of spices. The cuisine of this region is heavily influenced by the geography, climate, and history of the central Indian states. Iconic dishes of Central Indian cuisine include Jalebi, Samosa, and a variety of curries and gravies, often made with a blend of spices and ghee.

Rice and breads are also staples in Central Indian cuisine, and both vegetarian and non-vegetarian dishes are an important part of the cuisine. Central Indian cuisine offers a unique and exciting culinary experience to anyone who is interested in discovering the flavors and traditions of this region.

ϷϷϷ

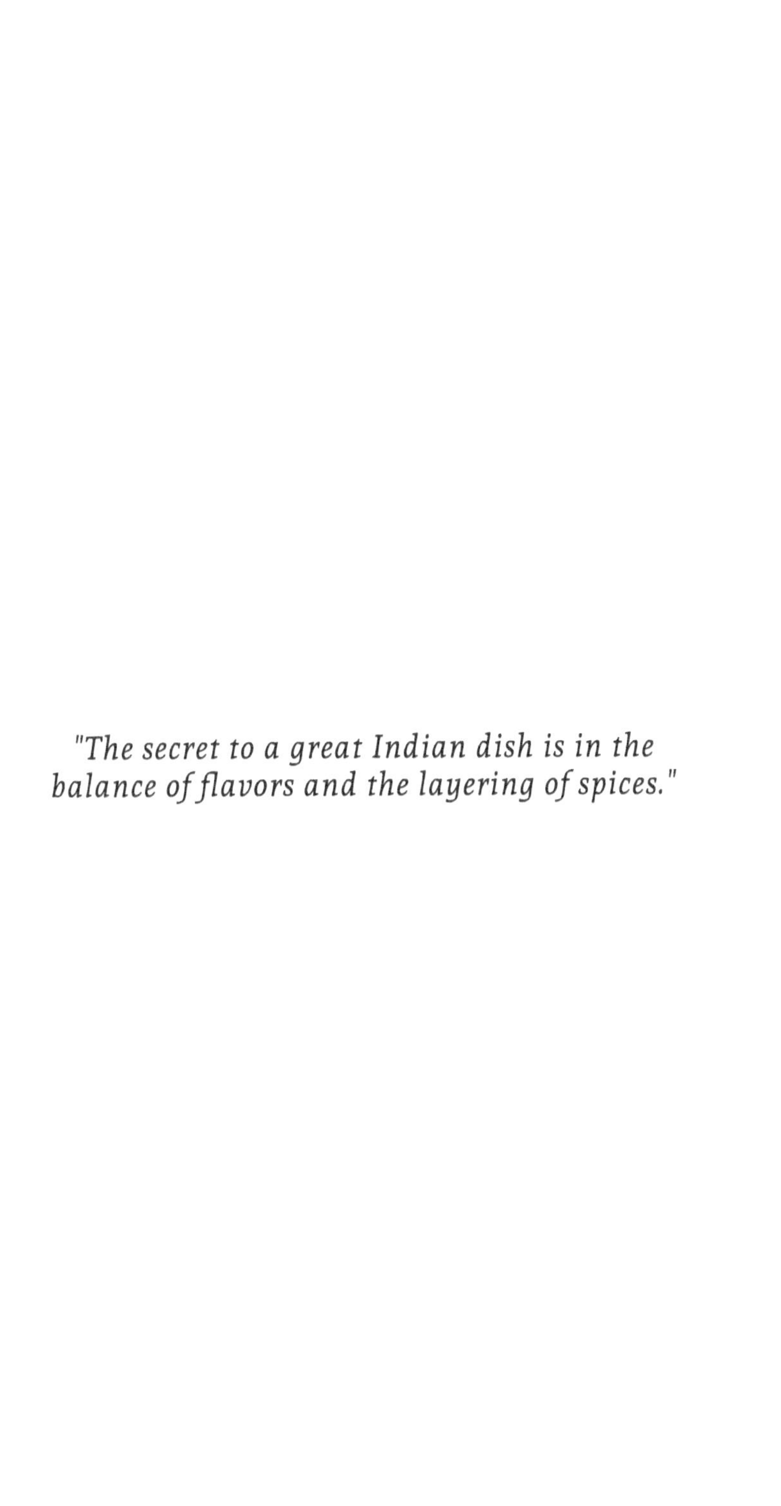
"The secret to a great Indian dish is in the
balance of flavors and the layering of spices."

SEVEN

THE EVOLUTION OF INDIAN SPICES AND SEASONING

The evolution of Indian spices and seasoning can be traced back to ancient times, when the Indus Valley Civilization developed a sophisticated system of agriculture and food production. Spices and herbs have played an important role in Indian cuisine for centuries, and have been used not only for flavor, but also for their medicinal properties.

In ancient times, Indian spices were highly sought after by traders and merchants from other parts of the world, who would travel to India to acquire these valuable spices. Some of the most popular spices of the time included black pepper, cinnamon, ginger, and turmeric.

During the Mughal Empire, Indian cuisine was heavily influenced by Persian and Central Asian cuisine, leading to the incorporation of new spices and seasoning techniques.

The Mughals introduced ingredients such as saffron, cardamom, and nutmeg, and also popularized the use of dried fruits and nuts in Indian cooking.

With the arrival of the British and the establishment of British colonial rule in India, Indian cuisine was further influenced by Western culinary techniques and ingredients. Indian cooks began to use new ingredients such as potatoes, tomatoes, and chili peppers, which were introduced by the British.

In recent years, Indian cuisine has undergone a resurgence in popularity, with an emphasis on traditional techniques and ingredients. Chefs and cooks are rediscovering the rich culinary heritage of India and are using these traditional spices and seasoning techniques in new and creative ways.

The evolution of Indian spices and seasoning can be traced back to ancient times, and has been shaped by a variety of cultural and historical influences. From the ancient Indus Valley Civilization to the Mughal Empire and British colonial rule, Indian cuisine has always been characterized by its rich and flavorful use of spices and herbs. Today, Indian cuisine continues to evolve, with a renewed emphasis on traditional techniques and ingredients, and an increasing interest in the rich culinary heritage of India.

ppp

"Indian cuisine is like a work of art. Each dish is a masterpiece, with its own unique blend of flavors and spices."

EIGHT

INDIAN STREET FOODS AND SNACKS

Indian street foods and snacks are an integral part of Indian culture, and are enjoyed by people of all ages and backgrounds. These foods are often quick, affordable, and delicious, and are an important part of daily life in India.

One of the most iconic Indian street foods is the "chaat", a popular snack that includes a variety of ingredients such as potatoes, chickpeas, yogurt, and tamarind chutney. Popular chaat dishes include bhel puri, pani puri, and dahi puri.

Another popular Indian street food is "vada pav", a sandwich made with a deep-fried potato dumpling, known as vada, served in a bun with a variety of chutneys and spices.

Indian street food also includes a variety of fried snacks

such as samosas, kachoris, and bonda, which are often served with chutneys or dips. Indian street food also includes a variety of sweet treats such as jalebi, gulab jamun and rasgulla.

In addition to traditional Indian street foods, there are also a variety of international street foods that have been adapted to Indian tastes, such as Chinese-style momos and pakoras, which are a type of fried fritter.

Indian street food is not only delicious but also affordable and easy to find. Street vendors can be found in markets, busy streets, and at fairs and festivals. They offer a variety of snacks and meals to suit all tastes, and are an important part of daily life in India.

Indian street foods and snacks are an integral part of Indian culture, and are enjoyed by people of all ages and backgrounds. These foods are often quick, affordable, and delicious, and are an important part of daily life in India. Indian street food include traditional Indian street foods and international street foods that have been adapted to Indian tastes. They are not only delicious but also affordable and easy to find, and are an important part of daily life in India.

"The variety of flavors and spices in Indian cuisine is a reflection of the diversity of the country."

NINE

India's Regional Drinks and Beverages

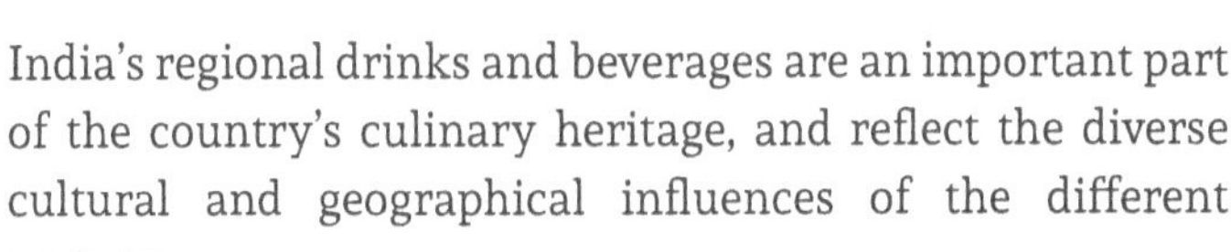

India's regional drinks and beverages are an important part of the country's culinary heritage, and reflect the diverse cultural and geographical influences of the different regions.

In the northern regions, popular drinks include lassi, a yogurt-based drink that is often flavored with spices or fruits, and sharbat, a sweet and refreshing drink made from flowers, fruits or nuts.

In the western regions, popular drinks include kokum sharbat, made from the kokum fruit and is commonly consumed in Konkan and Goa. Another popular drink is "sol kadhi", a refreshing drink made from coconut milk and kokum, which is often consumed to cool down the body during hot weather.

In the southern regions, popular drinks include filter coffee, a strong and flavorful coffee that is made using a traditional Indian filter, and "masala chai" a popular tea that is made with a combination of spices such as ginger, cardamom, and cloves.

In the eastern regions, popular drinks include "toddy" a fermented palm sap, and "chaa" a popular tea that is made with black tea leaves and milk.

Alcoholic drinks are also an important part of India's culinary heritage, with a wide variety of traditional beverages such as rice beer, palm wine and "Feni" a liquor made from cashew or coconut.

India's regional drinks and beverages are an important part of the country's culinary heritage, and reflect the diverse cultural and geographical influences of the different regions. Popular drinks include lassi, sharbat, filter coffee, masala chai, toddy and chaa.

Alcoholic drinks are also an important part of India's culinary heritage, with a wide variety of traditional beverages such as rice beer, palm wine and Feni. These traditional drinks are an essential part of India's culinary heritage, and offer a unique and exciting culinary experience to anyone who is interested in discovering the flavors and traditions of India.

ﭒﭒﭒ

"An Indian kitchen is a place where tradition meets innovation and flavors come alive."

TEN

THE IMPACT OF THE MUGHAL EMPIRE ON INDIAN CUISINE

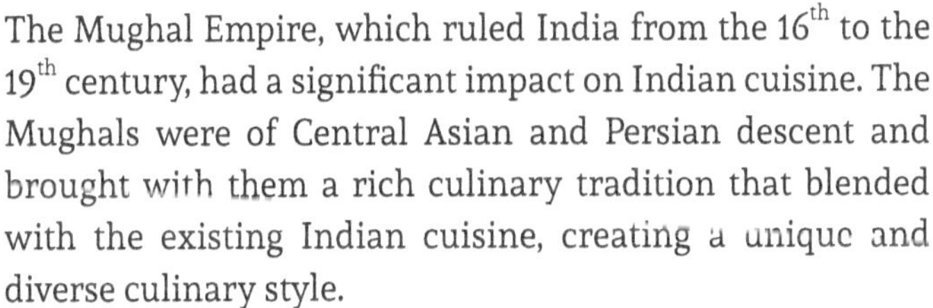

The Mughal Empire, which ruled India from the 16th to the 19th century, had a significant impact on Indian cuisine. The Mughals were of Central Asian and Persian descent and brought with them a rich culinary tradition that blended with the existing Indian cuisine, creating a unique and diverse culinary style.

One of the most notable impacts of the Mughal Empire on Indian cuisine was the introduction of new ingredients and cooking techniques. The Mughals brought with them a wide variety of spices and herbs, such as saffron, cardamom, and nutmeg, which are now commonly used in Indian cuisine. They also introduced new cooking methods, such as slow-cooking and roasting, which helped to create rich and flavorful dishes.

The Mughals also introduced a new culinary aesthetic, which emphasized the use of fruits, nuts, and dried fruits in cooking. This led to the creation of new dishes such as biryani and kebabs, which are now considered to be quintessential Indian dishes.

The Mughals also had a significant impact on the way food was served and presented. They introduced the concept of royal kitchens and elaborate banquets, which were characterized by rich, opulent meals and a wide variety of dishes. This had a lasting impact on Indian cuisine, and the tradition of serving a wide variety of dishes at special occasions continues to this day.

The Mughal Empire had a significant impact on Indian cuisine, introducing new ingredients, cooking techniques, and culinary aesthetics. The Mughals brought with them a wide variety of spices and herbs, and introduced new cooking methods such as slow-cooking and roasting. They also introduced the concept of royal kitchens and elaborate banquets, which had a lasting impact on Indian cuisine. Today, many of the dishes and cooking styles that were popular during the Mughal Empire continue to be enjoyed and have become an integral part of Indian cuisine. The Mughal influence can be seen in popular dishes such as biryani, kebabs, and biryanis, which are now considered to be quintessential Indian dishes. Many of the traditional Mughal dishes are still prepared and served in the traditional way, passed down through generations and are considered delicacies.

The Mughal Empire also had a significant impact on the way food was served and presented, introducing new culinary aesthetics and elevating the status of food and culinary arts. The Mughals were known for their love of food, and this was reflected in their opulent banquets, which featured a wide variety of dishes and were often accompanied by music and entertainment. The Mughals also introduced the concept of royal kitchens and the use of elaborate table settings and dishes made of gold and silver.

In addition to the introduction of new dishes, ingredients and cooking techniques, the Mughals also influenced the way food was consumed in India. They introduced the concept of formal dining and the use of cutlery, which was not commonly used in India at the time. This had a lasting impact on Indian cuisine and dining culture, and the tradition of using cutlery continues to this day.

The Mughal Empire had a significant impact on Indian cuisine. They introduced new ingredients, cooking techniques, and culinary aesthetics, which have become an integral part of Indian cuisine. Many of the traditional Mughal dishes continue to be enjoyed and have become an integral part of Indian cuisine, and the Mughal influence can be seen in the way food is served and presented in India. The Mughals also had a significant impact on the way food was consumed, introducing the concept of formal dining and the use of cutlery. The Mughal Empire's influence on Indian cuisine continues to be felt to this day, and is an important part of India's culinary heritage.

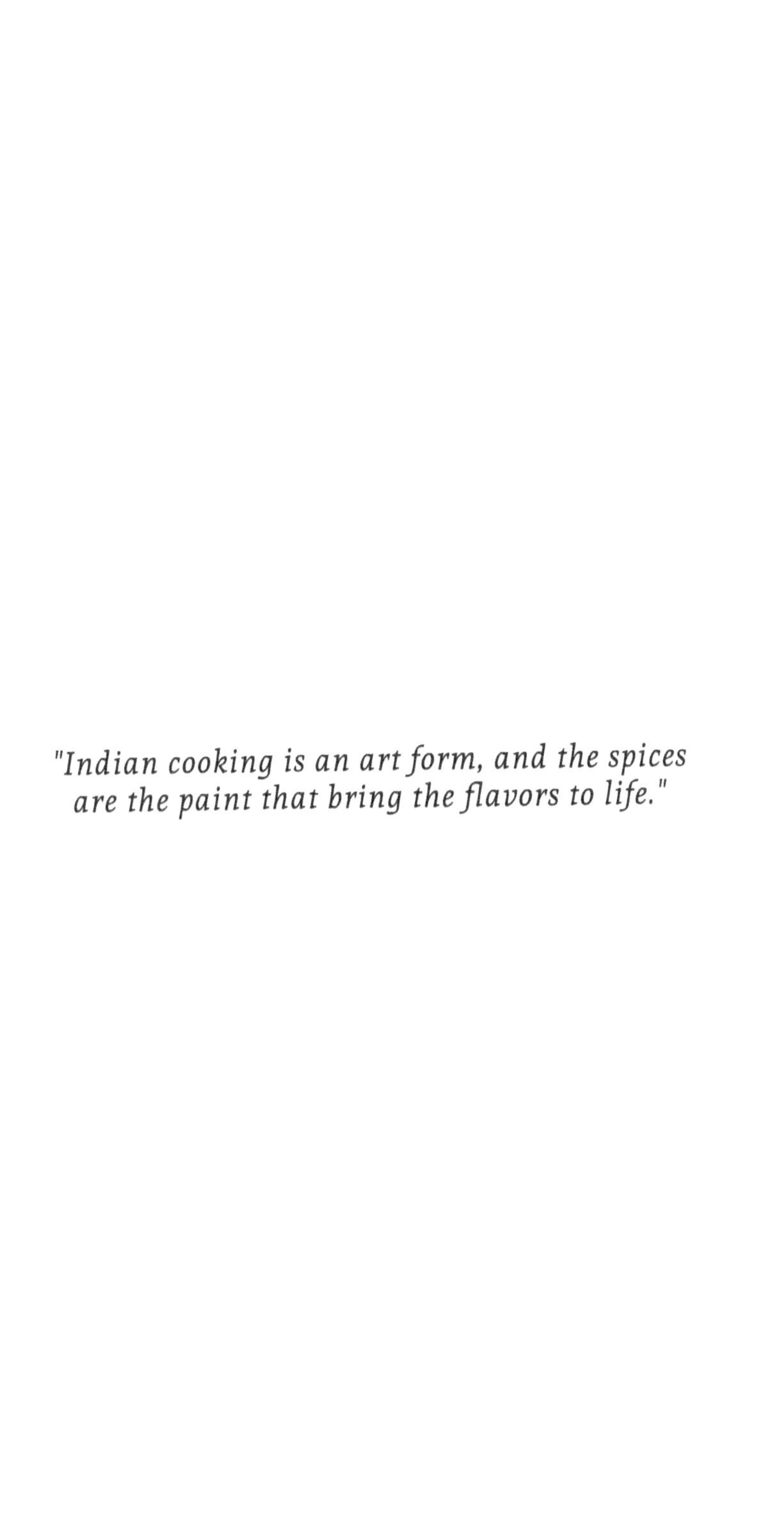

"Indian cooking is an art form, and the spices
are the paint that bring the flavors to life."

ELEVEN

INDIAN FOOD AND ITS INFLUENCE IN GLOBAL CUISINE

Indian food has had a significant influence on global cuisine, with its unique blend of spices, flavors, and cooking techniques. The popularity of Indian food has grown in recent years, with Indian restaurants and cuisine now found in many cities around the world.

One of the key ways in which Indian food has influenced global cuisine is through the use of spices. Indian cuisine is known for its use of a wide variety of spices, such as turmeric, cumin, coriander, and ginger, which are now commonly used in many global cuisines.

Indian cooking techniques have also had a significant impact on global cuisine. The use of slow-cooking and simmering, which is common in Indian cuisine, has become a popular method for cooking in many global cuisines. The use of yogurt and other fermented foods, which are common in Indian cuisine, has also become increasingly popular in global cuisines.

Indian food has also influenced global cuisine through the popularity of its street food and snacks. Dishes such as samosas, pakoras, and chaat are now commonly found in global street food markets, and have become popular in many countries.

Indian food has also had an influence on the development of fusion cuisine, which combines elements of different cuisines to create new and exciting dishes. Indian ingredients and cooking techniques have been used in fusion cuisine to create unique and flavorful dishes that are enjoyed around the world.

Indian food has had a significant influence on global cuisine, with its unique blend of spices, flavors, and cooking techniques. Indian cooking techniques, such as slow-cooking and simmering, and the use of yogurt and other fermented foods, have become popular in global cuisines. Indian street food and snacks have also become popular around the world, and Indian food has also influenced the development of fusion cuisine. Indian cuisine continues to inspire and excite food enthusiasts around the world, and its influence is likely to continue to grow in the future.

❧❧❧

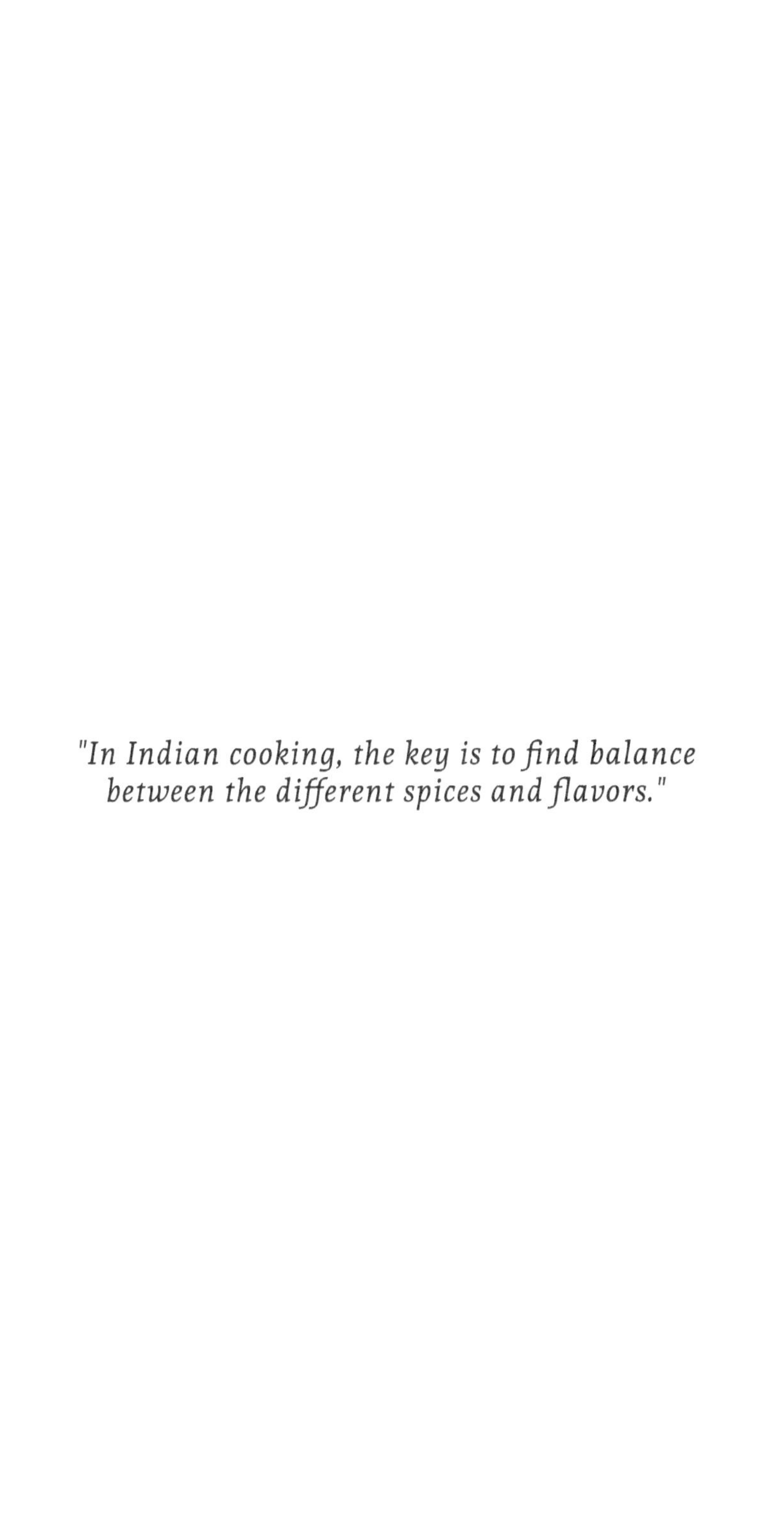
"In Indian cooking, the key is to find balance
between the different spices and flavors."

TWELVE

India's Regional Sweets and Desserts

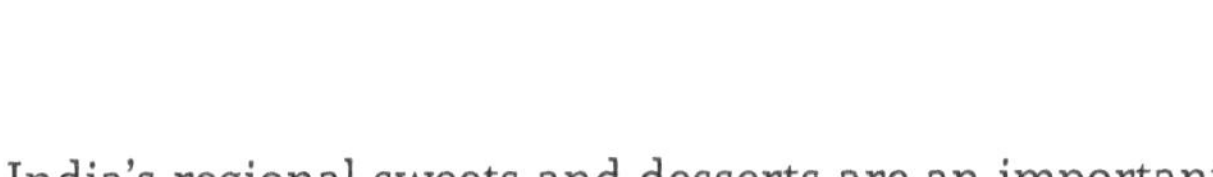

India's regional sweets and desserts are an important part of the country's culinary heritage and reflect the diverse cultural and geographical influences of the different regions.

In the northern regions, popular sweets and desserts include ras malai, a soft cheese dumpling served in sweetened milk, and gulab jamun, a deep-fried dough ball soaked in sugar syrup.

In the western regions, popular sweets and desserts include modak, a sweet dumpling filled with a mixture of grated coconut and jaggery, and shrikhand, a sweet yogurt-based dessert flavored with saffron and cardamom.

In the southern regions, popular sweets and desserts include payasam, a sweet pudding made with rice or vermicelli and flavored with cardamom and saffron, and Mysorepak, a sweet made of gram flour, ghee, and sugar.

In the eastern regions, popular sweets and desserts include rasgulla, a syrupy sweet made from chhena and semolina dough, and Kheer a sweet pudding made of rice and milk.

India's regional sweets and desserts are often made with a combination of traditional ingredients such as ghee, milk, and sugar, and are often flavored with a variety of spices such as cardamom, saffron, and nutmeg. They are also often served during festivals and special occasions, and are an important part of India's cultural heritage.

India's regional sweets and desserts are an important part of the country's culinary heritage and reflect the diverse cultural and geographical influences of the different regions. They are often made with a combination of traditional ingredients such as ghee, milk, and sugar, and are often flavored with a variety of spices such as cardamom, saffron, and nutmeg.

They are also often served during festivals and special occasions, and are an important part of India's cultural heritage. These traditional sweets and desserts offer a unique and exciting culinary experience to anyone who is interested in discovering the flavors and traditions of India.

᭼᭼᭼

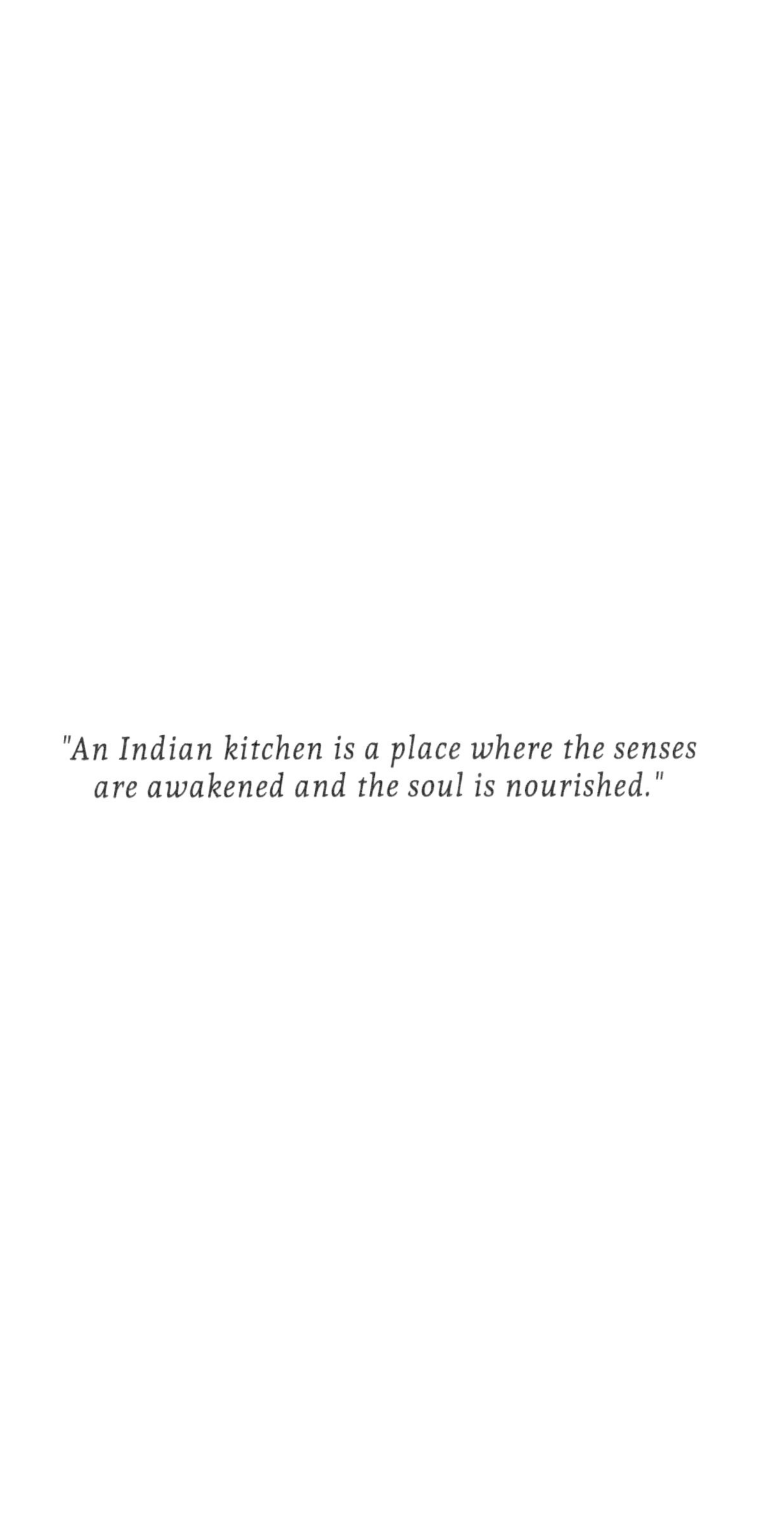

"An Indian kitchen is a place where the senses
are awakened and the soul is nourished."

THIRTEEN

INDIAN CUISINE AND ITS RELATIONSHIP WITH RELIGION

Indian cuisine has a close relationship with religion, with many traditional dishes and ingredients having specific religious significance. Hinduism, Jainism, Buddhism and Sikhism are the major religions in India and each of them has a unique relationship with food.

In Hinduism, food is seen as a way to connect with the divine and many traditional dishes are offered as prasad, or food that has been blessed by the gods. Additionally, many Hindus follow a vegetarian diet as a way of showing respect for all forms of life.

In Jainism, the practice of non-violence is applied to food choices and Jains are strict vegetarians and refrain from consuming root vegetables such as garlic, onions, and potatoes.

In Buddhism, food is seen as a means to nourish the body and support spiritual practice, and many traditional Buddhist dishes are simple and nutritious.

Sikhs also have a strong tradition of communal dining, and Langar, a free kitchen, is open to everyone regardless of religion, caste, color, creed, age, gender, or social status.

In addition to religious dietary restrictions, many traditional Indian dishes are also prepared and consumed during religious festivals and ceremonies. For example, during the Hindu festival of Diwali, traditional sweets such as Gulab Jamun, Ras Malai, Jalebi, and Rasgulla are prepared and consumed.

Indian cuisine has a close relationship with religion, with many traditional dishes and ingredients having specific religious significance. Each of the major religions in India has a unique relationship with food, such as vegetarianism and non-violence in Jainism, simple and nutritious food in Buddhism, and communal dining in Sikhism. Many traditional Indian dishes are also prepared and consumed during religious festivals and ceremonies, and are considered to be an important part of religious practice and culture.

ppp

"Indian food is a celebration of the senses, where flavors and spices come together in perfect harmony."

FOURTEEN

VEGETARIAN AND NON-VEGETARIAN CUISINE IN INDIA

India is known for its diverse cuisine, which includes both vegetarian and non-vegetarian options. Vegetarianism is a common dietary choice in India, particularly among Hindus, Jains, and Buddhists, who make up a significant portion of the population. Many traditional Indian dishes are vegetarian and are based on a combination of grains, legumes, and vegetables, often flavored with a variety of spices.

Non-vegetarian cuisine is also an important part of Indian cuisine, particularly in regions such as the North-East, coastal regions and the North-West. The most common forms of meat consumed are chicken, mutton, and fish. These dishes are often prepared with a variety of spices and herbs, and are enjoyed with a variety of breads or rice.

Both vegetarian and non-vegetarian cuisine in India are characterized by the use of a wide variety of spices and herbs, which are used to create flavorful and aromatic dishes. Indian cuisine is also known for its use of traditional cooking methods, such as slow-cooking and simmering, which help to create rich and flavorful dishes.

In addition, Indian cuisine also has a wide variety of street foods and snacks, many of which are vegetarian, such as samosas, pakoras, and chaat. These are enjoyed by people of all ages and backgrounds and are an important part of daily life in India.

Indian cuisine includes both vegetarian and non-vegetarian options. Vegetarianism is a common dietary choice in India and many traditional Indian dishes are vegetarian. Non-vegetarian cuisine is also an important part of Indian cuisine, particularly in regions such as the North-East, coastal regions, and the North-West. Both vegetarian and non-vegetarian cuisine in India are characterized by the use of a wide variety of spices and herbs, which are used to create flavorful and aromatic dishes. Indian cuisine also has a wide variety of street foods and snacks, many of which are vegetarian, and are enjoyed by people of all ages and backgrounds.

ppp

"Indian spices are like a love story, each one
has its own unique tale and together they
create a beautiful romance of flavors."

FIFTEEN

INDIA'S FAST-EVOLVING MODERN CUISINE SCENE

India's modern cuisine scene has been rapidly evolving in recent years, with a growing focus on fusion and experimentation. This new generation of chefs and restaurateurs is drawing inspiration from traditional Indian ingredients and techniques while also incorporating global flavors and cooking styles.

One of the most notable trends in India's modern cuisine scene is the rise of molecular gastronomy, which involves the use of scientific techniques and equipment to create unique and innovative dishes. This has led to the creation of new and exciting dishes that push the boundaries of traditional Indian cuisine.

Another trend in India's modern cuisine scene is the increasing popularity of fusion cuisine, which combines elements of different cuisines to create new and exciting dishes. This has led to the creation of dishes that blend Indian flavors with those from other countries, such as Italian, Chinese, and Mexican.

Additionally, there is an emphasis on the use of locally sourced and seasonal ingredients, and an increasing focus on sustainability and environmental responsibility in the restaurant industry.

There has also been a growing popularity of artisanal and craft food products, such as small-batch pickles, homemade chutneys, and artisanal cheeses. This has led to the emergence of a number of small-scale producers who are dedicated to maintaining traditional methods and using locally sourced ingredients.

India's modern cuisine scene is rapidly evolving, with a growing focus on fusion and experimentation. There is a rising trend of molecular gastronomy, fusion cuisine and the use of locally sourced and seasonal ingredients. There is also an emphasis on sustainability and environmental responsibility in the restaurant industry, as well as an increasing popularity of artisanal and craft food products. These developments are pushing the boundaries of traditional Indian cuisine and offering new and exciting culinary experiences for diners.

ᖚᖚᖚ

Other Books Of The Author

1. The Moments When I Met God
2. Kashiyile Theertha Pathangal
3. GURU GYAN VANI
4. Abhiprerak Gita
5. ASSI SE JAIN GHAT TAK
6. Hopelessness of Arjuna
7. The Soul and It's True Nature
8. Sense of Action (Karma)
9. Action through Wisdom
10. Action through Wisdom
11. THEORY AND PRACTICAL OF EVERY ACTION
12. LOGICAL UNDERSTANDING OF THE SUPREME
13. THE IMPERISHABLE SUPREME
14. Yatra Nishadraj se Hanuman Ghat Tak
15. Yatra Karnatak Ghat se Raja Ghat Tak
16. Yatra Pandey Ghat se Prayagraj Ghat Tak
17. Yatra Ranjendra Prasad Ghat se Dattatreya Ghat Tak
18. YaatraSindhiya Ghat se Gwaliar Ghat Tak
19. Yatra Mangala Gauri Ghat se Hanuman Gadhi Ghat Tak
20. Yatra Gaay Ghat Se Nishad Ghat Tak
21. MAA GANGA, GHATEN EVM UTSAV
22. Ganga Arti Dev Deepavali evam Any Utsav
23. Potentials of Digitalized India
24. VEDIC CONSCIOUSNESS
25. A Brief Introduction to Vedic Science
26. Kashi ke Barah Jyotirling
27. IMPACT OF MOTIVATION
28. Let's have a Milky Way Journey
29. Color Therapy in a Nutshell

30. Rigveda in a Nutshell
31. Yajurveda in a Nutshell
32. Samveda in a Nutshell
33. Atharva Veda in a Nutshell
34. Ayushman Bhava - Ayurveda
35. Srimad Bhagavad Gita and Upanishad Connection
36. Srimad Bhagavad Gita - an attempt to summarize each chapter.
37. Facts and Impact of Nakshatra
38. Astro Gems - NAVARATNA
39. Ekadashi - A Concise Overview
40. A Concise View of Hanuman Chalisa
41. Inspirational Gita
42. Nakshatraranyam
43. Summary of 18 Mahapuranas
44. Synopsis of 18 Upa Puranas
45. Rigvediya Upanishads
46. Shukla Yajurvediya Upanishads
47. Krishna Yajurvediya Upanishads
48. Samavediya Upanishads
49. Atharvavediya Upanishads
50. The Seven Great Sages
51. From Rocket Scientist to President Dr. APJ Abdul Kalam
52. The Visionary's Voice - Quotes of Dr. APJ Abdul Kalam
53. The Wisdom of Swami Vivekananda: Insights and Inspiration from a Legendary Spiritual Teacher
54. Ayurvedic Remedies from the Garden
55. Sages and Seers
56. Rising Strong – Motivational Stories of Women
57. Beyond Flames -Mystery stories of Funeral Ghat Manikarnika
58. The Origins of Tulsi: A Look at the Mythological Roots of the Plant"

59. The Holistic Cow: A Look at the Physical, Spiritual, and Cultural Importance of Cows in India
60. Arts of Healing
61. Exploring the Divine
62. Understanding Five Elements
63. The Etymology of Ram
64. Symbols of India
65. Voice of Change (About Speeches of Great Men)
66. She Speaks (About Speeches of Great Women)
67. Patriotism on Celluloid – Brief About Patriotic Films
68. The Music of Motivation: A Brief Guide to Inspirational Film Songs
69. Unlocking the Secrets of the Dashopanishads
70. A Cultural Mosaic
71. Ancient Traditions, Modern Minds
72. Ecos of Ancient Wisdom
73. Beneath the Surface
74. From Temples to Ashrams
75. Sages of the Subcontinent
76. The Art of Healling (Ayurveda, Yoga & Naturopathy)
77. The Indian Kitchen

❦❦❦

Contact

DR. JAGADEESH PILLAI

PhD in Vedic Science

Four Times Guinness World Record Holder

Winner of Mahatma Gandhi Vishwa Shanti Puraskar and
Global Peace Ambassador

Gemology, Astro & Vastu Consultant - Spiritual Counselor

Consultant for designing World Record Ideas

Efficient Tarot Card Reader

9839093003

myrichindia@gmail.com

drjagadeeshpillai@facebook

drjagadeeshpillai@instagram

jagadeeshpillai@youtube

www. JAGADEESHPILLAI.com

ᐅᐅᐅ

|| LOKAHA SAMASTHAHA SUKHINO BHAVANTU ||

• 73 •